ARCADIA, INDIANA

(a tragedy)

Arcadia, Indiana

Published by Plays Inverse Press
Pittsburgh, PA
www.playsinverse.com

ISBN 13: 978-0-9914183-8-1

First Printing: July 2017
Cover design: Ryan Spooner
Cover photo: Ben Altman, "The More That is Taken Away: Act 2, #11. Year 4, November."
Used with permission. For more information, please visit benaltmanphotographs.com
Page design: Tyler Crumrine
Printed in the U.S.A.

PLAYS INVERSE

ARCADIA, INDIANA

(a tragedy)

Toby Altman

PLAYS INVERSE PRESS
PITTSBURGH, PA
2017

Table of Contents

DRAMATIS PERSONAE *(the personated persons)*

• "Remember how bad it was yesterday? Here we go again." (Goldsmith)

Steelman: our hero. He is dressed in wounds: shattered lips and perjured eyes that open his tissues to business as usual.

Theas: Steelman's wife—or—what her name said. Her gender is like a badly-pasted poster, sloppily, incompletely imposed from the outside by anonymous hands. Beneath which: animate absence. A loose weave of nerve and brick.

Foreman: commodity, utility, fertility, beauty. He cultivates his appetites. He walks the factory in gray, permissive sweats. He stands his ground.

Wife: his dearly beloved. She is a fugue state: nothing pronounced as 'noting.'

Abominations: generic organic solids, dressed in tax.

Poet: a blank and wholesome face, masquerading as the law.

Verb: (his) weaponized language.

Toby: a principle of thrift, white and workmanlike. From his interminable prison in the lilacs, he texts the actors: u up ;-)

•

C.E.O.: death's second self. He bathes in streams of pink and silver resin to bind his carcass to itself. He sits over the vast factory floor, dove-like, brooding.

Chorus: board members at Arcadia Steel. They are respected, objective members of the community. They pass out luxurious wet and dry suckets, candied meats, and kissing confits to pacify the audience.

Reverend: he who reveres the end.

Shibboleth Places / Amorous Indigestion: good cop / bad cop.

Oedipus / Sphinx: the voice of reason / its victim.

Daddy: he vacuums all the pollution from my belly and leaves it here for the pleasure and edification of the consumer.

Dog: Tiresias in drag.

Congregants, factory workers, Arcadians (to taste).

ACT ONE

scene: Arcadia, Indiana, a company town. The act opens at Steelman's house. It is a perforated skin, endowed with winter filth. Later, we travel to the Bamboo Lounge, a tiki bar in the heart of Arcadia. Throughout the first three acts, the stage should be packed with pastoral trash[1] so thick that the actors must wade through it to enter and exit. Once onstage, they stand as still as possible, as though imprisoned by it. They do not make breathless mergers or peel away from each other. They call out as if issuing bureaucratic commands—especially in scenes of violence and sexual intimacy. At no point may one character touch another. Their hands hang at their sides like fat, yellow fish. They caress each other in the abstract parts of their blubber using an antiseptic idiom.

• *Argument:*

Enter our generic hero with a generic wound: in the foot like Oedipus or the ear like Hamlet. The precise texture and weight of his pain will not concern us here. This is a tragedy of liability and legality—a corporate pleasure for a corporate age. Let it suffice that he is breakage: the unknowable surplus of the workplace that Foreman (animated by generic appetites) must eliminate.

Out of work, pressed by need, Steelman foresees, foresuffers all: how Theas, his wife (generic medium between) will give tender slivers of herself to save their house and keep him on the job. How she will swallow Foreman's humoral mud, which catches in her stomach and seals it against grief. And yet, he turns his head from the merciful thing she meant.

---

[1] *car batteries caked in sugar; effervescent denture-cleaning tabs; crushed bags of Tostitos Scoops; Pampers and tampons; shattered sacks of chemical salt; royal oaks and cedars, murdered by invasive beetles; flavored condoms with the flavor sucked off; delicate, crumpled receipts; tax returns with the names redacted; the foam from a no-fat decaf latte; etc.*

ENVOY *(about the author)*

scene: live, from the bowels of Arcadia…

• *…the Poet sends an augury of his booty:*

Toby: I sing my self for sale: broke, butter-light,
and highly militarized. Once I drank
my song and ate it too. But Rumsfeld was right:
you go to war with the army you have.
Now, fragrant in not-things and fluent too,
pale Achilles walks his mother's roses.
Brittle as a grammar, man and his wound
sing together and pick each other's noses:

"Whoso sinks his sex in funeral meats,
some baked, some sweet, I know where is an hind,
left by holy buddies to stain the beach.
Do not touch him. He is Caesar's in mind,
  Circe's in body: go to him and write,
  'My love,'" (he coughs a rope of snot) "'is like:

• *about the author:*

Toby: Ok, excuse me while I ode myself—or what's left of me. Once I merged my delicate fingers with the internet, but its engine erupts aromatic paste, worn as prophylactic against the plague. Very soon I will be the silence of vespers. When the time comes, I'll draw my credit card like a flaccid sword and advance against the air. Hello, I am awed by all that is known: pale Iphigenia as she walks among her mother's roses. "Break forth unscented flesh in chives and bullion," (sez she, thru me). "Seedbed of the thing, sweetheart of the thing, break forth in salt and wisteria: the spring is here and dappled with its speculum."

He thinks he has an inalienable right to soda and sandwich—that this is what it means to be a man. Yet, under current political conditions such a desire is unspeakable as such. Therefore the skies blanch when he walks beneath them. The resources of his being are exhausted. There is no special augury in the fall of a sparrow. There follow three minutes of mortuary heat.

[exit Toby, permanently]

AUBADE *(o, bawd!)*

scene: Theas in the bath. Steelman sings her praises through the door. From a lofty pine beside the house, Foreman watches her in the suds, delighted.

•

Steelman:

I have always loved roses not always
since lady who verbs me all roses
will eat to a blank and lovely shape,
map of my urge, which against me closes.
One honey hour walked her waterways
and drink still the dark perfume of her thought.
One hour my mountainous spirit says,
"I investigate logistics of loss:
how my hand dissolves in embalming lotion
and frames the self among jubilant trees,
how you were caught, Achilles'd and ocean'd,
and now of earth and pleasure take your leave."
  The question was whether your savage breast
  would be savaged by art. Yes, I say, yes.

• *"I too was born in Arcadia."*

She steps from the bath, hair on her forehead oil-black, massed in tumorous braid: she does not answer. The dog paws the earth and samples the air: somewhere measure is broken. From his place in the pine, Foreman rejoices and sings the rupture:

Divine Theas, queen of the bath—she of the steak-thigh—she net of lace. Peel her pale skin: touch the tight-packed river-silt within. Lift the silt, like a sheet of wax: find a flock of angels, engaged in musical debate. Night and day, they feast upon the eye and spit the iris back. Hence the marbled plumpness of her breast, overstuffed with it. And yet, her fullness sets an absence in me. Her silence sets a music, which un-limbs, sends the fat to wander in itself: unmeasured, at last, undressed. So I will be: of essence cured and sex unstitched.

PROBLEMS OF BEAUTY (sparse rhyme)

scene: enter Foreman, fluid as time, to offer Theas his help. To praise the particular plumpness of her lips and no other. Her voice, light as beer foam. To say the substance, sublime, streaked by child:

•

Foreman:

So pluck it out if pleasure makes the eye
opaque: which I melts or eats itself or
sings the hours in the bush by your door,
O lady which is lunched in dark tree and sky.
In proof whereof, witness our Wyatt: knee
elastic as syntax, sings crooked body
(his and hers) in park and hotel lobby:
thus you are savage question and some me.
And witness the magnificent sparrow
as she gorges herself on lunch cancer.
Eat shit, sparrow—go on—eat the marrow
of eye and barf it back—there's your answer.
  But witness you, which excretes bird and tree.
  Prosecution rests: all this you far exceed.

•

In the wine-dark waters of her cell phone, the fishies say OOWHHooP OOWHHooP. And their words are pregnant with consent. "Listen," says Foreman, "to the ache—heavy with form—that populates your husband's wound. It says, *FUUNTZ BA BE O. FUUNTZ BE BA BITZE-O.*" Theas sighs, and shifts her weight. "Listen," says foreman, "Each of us must act his part in unknown languages. But your husband stretches past grammar, a voyager, sallied forth from the burnt coasts of the corpse. He is useless dough, unbound stone." The pipes shudder in protest: *SHRANRRRTZzzz SHRANRRRTZzzziee.* "I will not let him work again—unless you thrust your hand into my bowels and map me. For I am twenty-one, and full of luscious wind. For I watch you sweep the pages of Cosmo, and I see you linger on the sex tips." The dog shivers beneath the table, and growls: *MMM-MMM MAMMON.*

LANDSCAPE WITH WIND *(devoutly to be wished)*

scene: she consents.

• *"small talk: work and the weather."*

Theas:

I find I am a great many people
each one networking with the wind.
I find I am dressed in the scent of things:
severe and stormy—somewhat cheerful.
I find I am fragile as the weather:
weather that weather composes.
I find I am populated by roses,
bush of thought and dusky leather,
built by loss and thrilled by startled songbirds,
which rising choir I call "brutes,"
I call "exemplary bodies," call "use,"
since all at work with time, you launch your words
  from this table of wind and breast,
  which I call "certainty," call "rest."

• *Landscape with Abominations (devoutly to be washed).*

T: there was a car crash in my chest and all the Abominations died there was a grease fire in my chest and all the Abominations ate it and they smack their abominable lips and they do 1 hundred push ups with each of their 1 hundred tentacles *F:* i feed my tentacle with pancreas and snake just as the doctor said the weather is very fine yesterday the clouds came down in burial linen and blew their organs through my nose they blew pork chop and liver blew pancake and Froot Loops then they stopped blowing *T:* there was a car crash in my chest and my husband climbed out and massaged his wound there was a grease fire in my chest and the god of the Abominations eats it and blesses us and recites a litany of his convictions *that love occurs most in the deep bowels of a horse that it is conditional that wheat and mud shiver it that sex bark it* there is horse flesh in him fecund and the Abominations lick their heavy lips and the Abominations laugh and ask did you ever hear such a wind-fucker as this

FOLDING *(and unfolding)*

scene: later, in the back booth of the Bamboo Lounge, Foreman relates her to his friends. They were called, then, after the custom of the place, 'The Abominations.' And the Abominations grin and shake his hand, "Terrific," "Hey there, Stud," "Pray that thou mayst contain thyself."

•

Foreman:

She says, "The self is totally whether—"
Okay cookie. Then let's leave it at that.
Outside, language touches its black pleasure
tooth to the grass and draws up a few facts:
viz: the pungent blank on your underpants:
sludge of Metuchen, self-eating, self-made,
viz: the hot bath which makes your fanny blanch—
and still an absence makes you to its way.
"Most obvious about me is absence,"
she says. "Touch me with your tooth; I go mute.
Speak: I drain through like a punctured abscess,
and slurp the bitter juice from champagne flutes."
Are you first matter then, extension, weight?
"As the soul livest, Sir, I will not say."

•

[enter the Poet, with insufferable need]: Poetry makes nothing delicious. Makes a fragrant nothing: cool ranch of solitude, a way to mouth me. *[enter the Poet, with luminous tackle]:* This is a sorrow that bridges. This is a pasture fenced by flesh. This is a fence *[enter the Poet, with a purse of water and a Verb]:* O, there is a set of conditions. There are such things. There is no more unnatural nature or impiety knees. There is no more restraint. Limb the father, which is a fingerprint. Let the thing

[exit the Poet, with his gear; manet the Verb, with a poniard in one hand and a rope in the other]: We lost our way to grief. A handbook of water. The time was greaved and jointed. Hieronimo is, again. Love handle: sized to Mephistopheles, his bruised and margarine hands. "Leave me in a trance and so forth." "Hamlet, who deals in time." "If he hollers, let him go." "Close up the goggles of his sight." "Are we not great persuasions?"

SONG *(personal business)*

scene: she put her money where her mouth was: dread marks in her underwear and a belly full of rent. Still, he crackles like soda spilled on a sofa. "You can't have too much nothing," he says and winks, weary as the world.

She: In the spring, the ditches are ripe with cardboard and ruined cabbage: the style of desire particular to our era. I sought a prophylaxis against sorrow: an aperture, a tendon wrapped in wax paper. I point to my writing when my writing fails. The valley laced with ropes of hay and pasteurized lilacs. Unlikely beings who seem more alive, not less, when images are made of them. Would it be a trespass, then, to say that they look tellingly radiant in the flesh?

He: Not my problem.

She: "I realize there is a spaciousness inside me," said a woman on the bus. Then, "What I ask of writing is a very dusk seam. A fence, inanimate and nervy." I conceived a violent desire to be ill. I tried to purge myself of absence by drinking tumblers of hard water. Still, at the fulcrum of hunger, I open into a formal feeling: clean and particular, a logical architecture.

He: Not my problem.

She: I use the idiom of appetite as I find it. It is luscious with its legs together, luscious apart:

a wedge
of wet
tissue

in the small
of the back,

through which
the poem
asserts
its brute

geometry.

It is a laundry for abstraction, full of matter and pointing past it. It is a vegetable substance gathered in the blank places and rotting. Being so complex and vascular, so touched in the bower of bone, it is the give in the crotch of an old pair of jeans, the secret remnants of lilac and gum in the folds of the couch. It is the ache or its architecture. It settles in the hollow parts of things and yanks them back. It is the past with its tendons in a twist.

He: Not my problem.

[He is the hardness in hearing, the drag in time. He mutters to himself, "Whatever. Never mind." He rises from the couch and preps his wound—whatever it is—for work.]

ACT TWO

scene: male bonding on the floor of Arcadia Steel. In the distance, the towers of the steel mills are gently manifest, belching their aqueous fumes which adhere to the audience and actors and perfume them with rotten soda.

• *Argument:*

Pale and savage, he dresses in the dark, fumbling with his belt and socks. Then, on the floor of the factory, he announces to Foreman: "I am the very place of exile, that is, the place of the absence of place, the place of dispersal." And Foreman answers, "I trafficked in signs of fractured time. I became part of the ruin. I am refusal to say: nick and nack, paddy-whack, on her burnished throne."

There is wild grass between them, quiet, capacious, and warm. There are the limits of the flesh which are knit together like the laces of a boot. And there is the hand (I will not say whose) which unknits them.

PIG IRON BALLET *(a style of joy)*

scene: the floor of the factory. Foreman calls his men to work.

•

Foreman: Jug boys, hum boys, and strike the tambourine,
so tympanum and drugged, so smooth and spun:
of flat forehead and pasteboard mask, of meat
and matter cleaned. Raise the steel, strike the drum.

Steelman: Three years I struck the drum and then the drum
struck back, and shattered nape and nerve.
When drunk with steel and tar, I stood and strummed
my sinews raw, didn't I swerve—
didn't I carrion—didn't I come—
went down and wept by River Calumet—
run soft, run sweet, till I end my wounded song.

Chorus: We've heard too much: such sinew in your stom-
ache argues fragrant mud, a rough, fresh sex—
rise to the drum and find an end to song.

• *notes:*

Let me rehearse the things we know: (1) sometimes one asks the spine and breast to dissolve in language. Here is a wounded man, ruined by work. Strip his leathers and wash his back. Bring him coffee and a bowl of soup. (2) One may ask how the corpse is sculpted. And one may expect, at last, an answer from the governing angels, exhausted and resentful: "Out of bitter. Out of bullion and onion. Three parts water, one part stone."

(3) The prisoner must sing at the time of his circumcision, in pureness and boredom. (4) So it is with all about: sublime and tedious to think at all. Tedious and sublime, but good enough to walk around. To take an afternoon coffee with a little cream; to walk the metered earth and say to it: "That I might see, and know, and yet abstain: therefore I am still, though absence police the edge of me."

HOMILY *(supposé savoir)*

scene: Steelman, on the line, discourses of his wife—her silence, her rented tents, her mechanisms in festival season: "He is supposed to know that from which no one can escape...quite simply, signification."

• *"Secret grief is a cannibal of its own heart."*

Steelman: The body is the frame which sets the word
to work in things. It digests what it thinks:
the living water lodged in touch; its hurt,
a salve, a temper, husked. I will not think it.
In visions of the night, I serve a seam,
a silence, house of clay. It eats the thorns
and dust. It rejoices when its hard seed
is split and swallowed up, unforged, unforced.

Chorus: Unreconciled: a secret grief here works
its paper hand between the saw and steel.
It will cut and cannibalize your word,
will strip your sinew for its noonday meal.

Steelman: Then wear me to the sinew, blank and sheer.
Work grief, numberless grief: unword me here.

• *Stage directions:*

Exit all weather at once—exit thread and cable song—exit the eating ocean—exit the hand which eats the ocean and comes back spelt—exit the grammar of self, fungible and raw—exit substance, bound by law—exit shape and god thereof—but leave the carcass on a bare stage. What will we name that which remains? A stone. An ache. A fringe. A lapse. Each of these call, separately, *grief*. Sing its magnetic potency. It makes an itch in the lungs. It makes the mouth. Then it makes the mouth heavy with speech. It fences us with skin. It unfences with the word. It draws the coats of the flesh tight against its essence. It means, "god is gracious." It means, "meaning is an incident of great beauty." It bursts the senses from their barren seams. It touches the stomach of things—wild and sudden. We cannot call it back. "Listen," says Grief. "This is the season of your unstitching."

A NULL (or, purgation)

• *Enter Steelman, in a frenzy, "doing metaphysics."*

Steelman: What is the thought which works inside the will
and lays its paper hand between the steel and saw?
It is the wakeful fire, which eats its fill
of death, perplexed, and binds it with the law.

• *Enter Steelman with a dismal kind of music.*

Steelman: Come, beat the genital drum, skeleton—
the god of shape is gone. Come cataract
in pasteboard mask and purge yr sex of song:
poor skeleton!—where you were is pulp and lack.

• *Enter Steelman in a shroud of ice.*

Steelman: Steelman set your house in order,
brine your lips with toilet water—
Steelman wash your milky dugs
with scented wax and spicy drugs.

• *Enter Steelman, pregnant with his own persistence.*

Steelman: A stone persists. An ache. A way of thought.
"bla bla bla," says the fire, "um, so what?"

• *Enter Steelman, pursued by self.*

oniranfertherockeyplaces
its discovery makes
a vastly eerlar,-oed
perspective indeed if one
to procure. Providence. the provider suspects it was
this "spiritual revenue" the heavenly store
on a pillar of dollars: keeper Aloh "the supreme
vicotrolo / cat o' nine tails servant of men
who want to get on"

doubtless now couched in a corner of the bamboo
lounge with fizz and gin raw strawberry cream
pleasure makes the skin transparent Foreman sees
the city in her plazas and shops where drunks sell
broken watches

a mood blared by trumpets, trom-
and qualify the bleak "size and ar-
bones, saxophones and drums,
rangements"

a song with turgid, inadequate words : to dress the hair in
mind and manure to lift the drooping head and yet,

the goat shivers as though strummed by an invisible hand
and bares its throat for song—

RHAPSODE *(of unsewing)*

scene: the floor of the factory.

• *Foreman and Steelman debate their joint stock:*

f: surcharged of juice and sinewed bruise.
s: asparagus in thrust. two throats, one ache.
f: the merciful thing she meant. rough stomach.
s: the narrow circle of. sinewed bruise.
f: a digression of air. her oceanic.
s: things we are obliged to think. cold space tied.
f: she bring me to my full. two throats, one eye.
s: the narrow circle of. her oceanic.

f: and as you are undivided country.
s: and as I house the layers of you in thought.
f: and as there is speaking in you, a cough.
s: and cleave to you. and make two less in me.
  s: being made in your shape. a governance.
  f: teach me your heaviness. teach me distance.

• *Enter the Poet with slaughtered wood.*

p: *Rhapsodos*—a specialist in stitching, *or*, the navigation of stone, *or*, anxiety. From the Greek, "dears and darlings." Invested in the tight proprieties of surgery. *i.e.* "With ravishing sound of his melodious harp." If all else fails, Mr. Poet, go out and crouch in the swamp. There, consumed with sudden mud, thinking finds its end. Not succession or lines of descent—contagions, epidemics, the wind. The Verb, an absent thing: tough jelly slathered in stone.

• *Enter the Verb, the majesty of dislocation.*

v: Ladies and Gentlemen, we all know this man, or someone like him. *[points at the Poet with a single slaughtered finger]* He slips on his gas mask and steps out of the bath. He takes a long drink of debt and smacks his lips. He comes to me nightly in a bikini and a Bill Clinton mask. He wipes the slime from his eye and slurps it back through a curly straw. He rises to his poems like a fat man to strawberry pudding. Luxurious solvent in which all human dissolves: before this pink plaster, he is succulent lip and shuttered tooth. Nothing else.

B A B E L *(20 seconds of cavernous drum)*

scene: he stabs him.

•

"oh yes" "doubtless" "did he?" "the substance of"
"sounding there" "was moonlight" "an obstruction
of the bowel" "how are you?" "I'm" "sage brush"
"to and fro" "in" "this bliss" "and intention"
"let the thing" "unmanure" "or" "unbranch"
"loathsome bough" "blissful lamp" "yes I'll" "do it"
"relentless are mine ears" "well said, old lance"
"drawn by the influence of her lights" "I split"
"even then" "she was a foreign country"
"soft now" "solemn" "a kiss upon the brow"
"he becomes the thing he thinks" "I'm hungry"
"for sorrow" "it withers, so" "like" "a vow"
    "torn" "taken" "at the mouth" "go down" "go down"
    "soft" "river" "sap" "to the slaughtering" "ground"

• *notes, banal and clinical:*

"This is another poem which attracts the wrong kinds of solemnity" "A balance of proportions and tones" "Which calm pleasure overflows" *[Here the thought splices: hand and drum, discernable by their saying.]* "Thus it is we…who are aware of certain poignant contaminations" "The most contracted of spaces" "Wild above rule or art" "The small circle of living matter" "Enormous bliss" *[Here the subject becomes indistinguishable from the drum. aaaaAAAAaaaa, says the drum. aaaaAAAAaaaa, says the subject.]* "She is a meteorological freak" "A wilderness of sweets" "She is mistletoe on the trunk of her father" "An unterrestrial meteor" *[Here the Poet in the wood is an inverted tree. A seeming essence of subtle air. We know him by the absence of drum, which the hand becomes.]* "The flesh is a tempest" "a form of time" "You may think it…but only briefly"

SONG *(commercial break)*

scene: the Poet licks his symptom and grooms his urge for a long, dogmatic slumber. The poem makes ready for his jelly. Farewell! Bon voyage! He goes delicate as a dumpster, celibate as a dumpster, into that good night. Probably for good.

Poet: I have seen personal pizzas, white and gray. "Who's gonna eat the sorrow off us?" they demand. Good thing I was born with the appetite of a major corporation! In my loins, it is still the time of year when the dead go door-to-door, selling evening. (Don't be alarmed. I'm a stay-at-home mom.) "The muse rolls deep with us" the dead vaunt. This is their company chant:

A pain is little lawns of milk
with music in the grass:
cold pastoral in the mouth
which captures what it lacks.

And all throughout a threaded eye
could give its revenue to you:
try Venereal Linen (trademark) today,
at the ghostly heart of food.

Many people, just like you, speak of waffles but in a dialect that sounds like death. In the winter when the moon is pinched, you wear apostrophe in your breast. What you want is to have the author and eat him too. "Take the tequila from woman's mind," you demand. Alas, the author is unavailable for comment. The dead answer on his behalf:

The language is a frail ballot,
a glass of milk without the glass.

It gives under pressure
its absence to the grass:

the thing and its suburbs
armored against all sex.

ACT THREE

scene: just in the nicks of time, here comes Grief, captain of corporeal industries, with all her delicious machinery.

• *Argument:*

logistics of the corpse. how to praise it. how to comb it and shave it as its specific absence slips away. how to carry it. how to dress it in its own bare remnants. how to judge its repeated ocean, repeated in song. how to test the distance of its water from itself.

how to know
the distance of
the poet's needle
from itself:
repeated ocean
in repeated song.
being many,
seeming one:
pierced
by the poet's needle
and still unstrung.

SHUDDER *(and lament)*

scene: Foreman in his death agony.

•

Foreman:

Helpless now, I was covered with slime
moving softly / glitter / The Hill / leaning
its back. Memory of our long talks:
agree on wetlands and / creeps bliss when sinking.
Flu-dust kinetic / lightwave / leach / protect
our non-physical kind / and all throughout
water nursing a helpless now / private
the cross / beatitude / agree about.

I was the most loved. I was the most loved.
I love the most hopelessly, sink this one.
The flowers, things / on circumstance / above:
last season, several horse / a drowning sum.
  It means / of persistence: / it is a help
  lessness, we know / we know / it is / a help.

• *notes:*

Chorus: The space where you were / persists: / rock / spindle / shear / engaged in the sod. / Each alike in this: / unfolded, they bear / a living mind.

Chorus: Happily, language is a thing. Happily, language is made of uneasiness. A pulse beneath the ribs that radiates melancholy. And your voice, when you let it, is the plow that broke you: to spindle and shape. Proserpina with her snakes.

Chorus: You could not remain / here, darling. / You were translated / to another air, / and cried, "to Heaven, / my love, to heaven, / and leave / you in the storm."

Chorus: The dog has left his shrine. In pious silence he trots the fields, nose down, hunting for a trace of urine. But the secret roads of the earth, which the gods traveled without motion or heat, have closed. And the backbone aches inconsolably.

VISCOUS CINEMA *(from first principles)*

scene: at first, Steelman, suspended over the corpse.

later, Foreman's Wife, suspended over the [ ]

• *Elegy (with emerging voices):*

Steelman: Here I raise the question of a garden:
the rows of honeysuckle and primrose
where longing gathers, epicene and cold.
How do we say its manure and burden,
which linger in the saying: some wet matter—
a viscous apricot, *exacted here,*
or Eros *the nerve-worn,* *sublime mirror* *who clears*
error *where it* *pressures to know* *the holly?*

Chorus: Here we raise the question of a garden:
April ocean and insatiable folding.
How do we know *this storm of withholding,*
this freight of length, this wife laid in tarnished
water and exacted here? down down hysteric soil
(she says) the sense aches *cypress / burdock / bitter / toil*

[*exit Steelman, pursued.*]

• *Dumb show (from first principles):*

(1) Presumably, the breath—not the word—was first: the latent everywhere. The wild wealth of the rock. (1.1) Adam's eating made a kind of nothing. He took a syrup of absence and fit it to his voice. (1.2) The mechanism of which resides in me: the subtle engine of sorrow at work, again, in the rough stubble of skin. (1.2.1) I fold in the object which feeds my sight: uncompromising spine; fruitful river in the eye.

(2) And yet, there is a certain spirit, or what our painters call air, which is seen in the face and especially the eyes. (2.1) e.g., how the hinge of metaphor is incarnate song—the voiceless ribbon of muscle as it unwinds into succulence, or symptom, or thread. (2.2) Each becomes the thing we think.

(2.3) Thus, I see a grammar—which comes after grace in the mechanics of things. It is just past the April of its age. (2.3.1) I comb its etc. And here's the juice of it: lament, placebo, or lil bo peep in it. [*This is the space of politics.*]

(3) [*This is the stuff of politics. / The stony center of his [ ] is / superflux. It lacks / an organizing music / which supplies / the specificity of objects.*] (3.1) Troublesome bladder: they gather it up. They leave the factory. And they name his battered [ ] in the streets: "~~wild mustard~~," "~~burdock~~," "~~bitter~~."

(3.2) Then, fragrance. (3.2.1) Then, the fragrance of loss / Foreman's Wife. (3.3) They lay him on her hearthstone for her to bathe and bury. (3.4) [*am i the organ / through which / He stiches and / unstitches*] (3.5)

[*Catastrophe is*
the possibility of return:
]

(4) It begins in self-division. (So it is sustained.) (4.1) Henceforth she remains, a mortar. Three months a wife, her husband is / astonished yew. Error in the knot. The natural state of the country. (4.2) In such synthesis, the labor ends. (4.2.1) She plunges her hand into [ ] and displays—where the eye was—an insoluble hole.

(5) Being what it was required to show.

• *Elegy (for first principles):*

Wife: Unclothed, you were the thing itself:
sovereign plaster, luxurious wet.
Unclothed, your breath was first landless:
a brace of salt, good to think with.
Now you are clothed again in sense,
syrup and shingle, glue of shape,
which takes your [ ] as a fence
[*troublesome bladder / full of wind / an animal space.*]

Chorus: Being so enraged—mare/mere/milk—
you leaked a length of perjured silk.
Being so mastered by the air,
you wore [*wild mustard, great with child*] in your hair.
Being so exacted here, you
[*who my chaste muse will not name. Besides, the rent is due.*]

DOUBTING THOMAS *(an anatomy)*

scene: Foreman's house; his Wife at work upon his absence.

• *She puts her finger in his side.*

I shaped him to his urn—
the fabric from his flesh—
the pliant thing in him—
I answered his urgency—
I shaped him a world
I showed him how to fold
and he walked the secret roads—
spikenard and shoulder bone—
and he took on breath
And yet the thistle is here—
unfungible
and yet he is mortared
by hair and fat
when scrubbed to blank
when shorn of word
remains an unsayable—

I peeled
I sculpted
to pleasure glass—
with liquid sighs—
of hand and day—
it in his frame—
and he drank
and he thickened—
from his unfenced.
flood-proved
and clear—
to himself
and gristle—
and essence—
and muscle—
to be buried—a seam—

• *Foreman [in distinct] discourses of his absence:*

I became a slave to the pure faculty of seeing.
This was the first cause of injury to my eyes.
None of these defects slackened my assault upon knowledge.
I wanted to be violently transformed by a stranger's touch.

I do not care for the depths of the flesh.
It is a form of haunting: muteness and minerality.
Here I am at the end of thinking.
I walk and walk in the unripe season.

Last year's grass is a visible darkness.
I know myself only as a fixture of the landscape.
The eye is a foreign language.

You see me deprived of my native music.
I take a crust of black bread to steady my milk-heave.
There is no origin of sorrow: only the warm approach

ESSAY *(on ordinary language)*

scene: Theas learns the news.

• *She puts down the phone, emboweled as the mountain.*

Chorus:

She takes a beer to steady her mouth.
Then she is beer foam / unclothed and / damasked.
Then she is the glass / 'whom love doth windlass.'
A place for loss. / A flight of milk. / A bout.

Chorus:

She comes with a black eye and uncorks it.
Then she is *the* *as* thermos and tulip,
each voracious for [ ] and how we know it:
wild in the grave, lilac and wish.

Theas:

At my back, I always hear stellar wind
and savage acre: love's winter liver—
each voracious for breach in the river,
or sensuous concrete *homo* *resin*
who moves in a medium she makes:
the world is all that is in case.

• *Coda (on language):*

It began in self-division. It delighted in boundary: anchored denture / where / a great cohesion arose.

Its aspect was such that all who looked upon it became silence. It was thought or bruteness of nature.

It was the frail, weary weed in which we dressed.

It was the distance in desire, which spilled soap into soap, compulsively.

It was the passage of joy: hurt plastic, overcome with sweetness.

It was the almond eye of heaven / vacant mood / rigid weather / when it branches in its dish.

It sang restraint: harness and stone, black hair, small hands, in sharp, urinous air.

It was lifted and cancelled by the burden that bent it.

It began in self-division. So it is sustained.

S O N G *(arcadia, indiana)*

scene: the matter he chiseled shrugs and gives up—"Thy silence then, that voices thee!"

slouched, slack
coal-black

Abel with
liquid

spits
wet-black

in back
where

wild blight
mud-drowned

ram and ewe
cold, liquid hour

tobacco wad
chewed-tight

frozen hedge
no one else will see.

•

He stayed three days, sleeping by the fire.
On the third day, Adam led him out
to the fields to draw his discourse
away from the house—since that fragrant voice,
dolorous voice, engenders a sweetness
in the loins, ivory in the waters,
"not proper to children…"
There, in the chaff, Adam asked:
"Stranger, what country are you from?"
And Adam answered in another voice,

[11 lines redacted here]

•

And Adam, always eager to know
the minds of angels:
"It must wear out. It must wear. Say, Angel,
by going up and down the field,
with mattock and hoe.
Say I will wear this earth away
to its essence. Say we will starve among the trees,
lords of ourselves and lords of our trash,
crazed, dizzy, but cleansed of our need."

ACT FOUR

scene: the rigorous cabinets of the law. The stage is implicit with lawyers and police, dressed in pastoral splendor: wreathes of holly and myrtle, dark cashmere jackets, well-pressed khaki slacks. The trash which both chokes and cherishes the stage has begun to dissolve and ferment. It resolves to a fine mud, a bubbly liquor—fresh as champagne, heavy as liquid plastic. The action is played with this juice sloshing around the actors' ankles. At times, the representatives of the law bend down to drink from it and lift their beaming lips, exultant.

• *Argument:*

The police get what they need from Steelman and bury the rest. Meanwhile, their lawyers patrol the streets of Arcadia, advertising the dulcet dawn of emergency law:

you may turn on
your cellular devices
you may lather
your hands in
antibacterial soap
and moisturizing
lotions
you are permitted
to know, carnally,
the supple ridge
of your armchair
perhaps you will agree
these are
exceptional freedoms

SUBPOENA *(the great writ)*

scene: idle chatter in the Arcadia police station. Sergeant Shibboleth Places explains to his partner, Officer Amorous Indigestion, how, as a boy, he and his brothers staged some inquiry on the status of the body: whether, like language, it is a thing; whether, like language, it is made of uneasiness. But now he says, with Goethe, "the best thou canst know thou mayst not tell to boys."

• *'some inquiry'*

S.P.:

We cut the earth with silver spades
to break the vault where my grandmother lay.
When we lifted her, naked in the air,
 I asked her, "Grandmother, say where
  the souls of the dead gather
 when they're still fresh, sharp as a radish—
 where they haunt before they vanish,
  stiff soles and broken bladders."

She replied, "I keep a silver dagger
in the pocket of my blouse to answer
 you with a wet and fluent sound:
 I raise it now against my mouth—
For you, I lay out the houses of health.
 I take the wound upon myself."

•

A.I.:

I take the wound upon yourself,
 I taste the houses of your health.
Such houses swarm with militant angels
and storms their flesh at the dinner table.
  "Let my people go," they sing
  and scrape the floor with their wings.
 "Love, careless love," they sing and blush:
  careless in love, pregnant as dust—
my doves! My Egypt! My sparrows!
"All language is echo," says Pharaoh
and slurps his beer, sly and insincere.
"Echo of what? Echo of what," he sneers.
They call him sermon, call him pointless bliss:
 I disagree. The point is this—

[enter Steelman, bound by law:]

Q U E S T I O N *(and answer)*

scene: the gentle officers have a few questions for their prisoner.

• *"However, I stand for 8-10 hours A day. Why is standing limited to 4 hours?"*

what moves in the I / I / what gives its shape /
its shape / what labors in its circle
to give its circle weight / its weight / what takes /
it takes / takes what / it takes its fertile
what / takes where / its where, dredged to the crisis /
does the crisis decide its fullness /
its fullness is the early fruit / violence
in his diet / which breaks the illness /
disdain of corpse for itself / what self /
sweet self / or sour self / the self that moves /
moves where / the fragile lens and the eye's depth
move / into what / into moving / for whom /
for moving, which makes its fortress in you /
for what / to make a space of I in you /

• *Principles of interrogation. To be projected throughout the scene:*

He may be forced to stand, to defecate
standing, until he collapses.
He may be forced to irrigate
his bladder until its content passes.
He may be beaten on the back and waist
with a regulation baton.
He may be isolated for thirty days
without food to force confession.

Deprive him of his religious comforts
and auditory influence.
Deprive him of light. Deprive him of slumber
by administering stimulants.
Remove his clothes. Force him to shave his hair.
And bind his hands behind a folding chair.

[When they have examined his case thoroughly and carefully, the officers return Steelman to his cell.]

ARCADIAN RHETORIC ( )

• *scene: having tasted the law, Steelman unthreads himself, permanently.*

Steelman:

Tomorrow is insatiable April:
the ruined ear expressing in broken
its voluptuous water. The fatal
grass, replete with you, which opens
a sharp misgiving in the tendon
and turns into torment and weariness:
mansion of form, tender and deep engine
that moves in nature to shape its less.

Still, I did not know desire: its dressing
in the dark. Its plastic craft. Brewing coffee
in bank and lung of the river. Its dwelling
in things where things unrest. For a body
  where April was spacious (and its lack),
  the question is: how to use pleasure as

[he dies.]

• *scene: et in arcadia ego.*

Ego:

Is he unfolded, this poor, foreclosed creature,
fraught with there is and heavy with forget?
Still, the harmony of his young compass
persists: a little milk to house the flesh.
And where he was: a ledge of nerve,
a swelling in the grass, still charged with breath
and dressed in sour curd of his inward,
where love and I rest, April-heavy and wet.

Do I know the body now? I know its
loss: how love makes a sonorous nothing
dusk and stubborn, dome of man-colored glass.
Its language lingers in the eye, pregnant
with pleasure. Crushed. Love was so early in us.
No writing can repair it. Love was so
evening in us. No thinking can frame its
exhausted making to song again.

How do we know the after making? "Making,"
he said, "the tent of blackberries in which
your sex is dressed. I sing its loss, its lack:
incessant oil, massaged into music.
Now if flows out of our hands and becomes
delicious reading: nothing without not,
thought without thinking, hugely politic,
exact in love. I find no trace of it."

ARCADIAN CHAMPAGNE (statements and facts)

scene: a press conference. The C.E.O. of Arcadia Steel lays his obligatory bouquet for the fallen boys.

• *Disclaimer:*

C.E.O.:

Then swerved the work and all the mergers failed,
and poets with their fudgy numbers wept
as credit cards capsized from the mail.
Still the derelict corporation slept—
slept in the high immaculate presence,
the silence, of the invisible hand,
a sudsy head of clear, cleansing resin:
wild money, which sweeps the yuck from the land.
O the minty-fresh glades where he branded
his brother with jellied petroleum
will be expungèd with a sterile hand-
towel and paved with cooked linoleum.
  Our lawyers agree: we dispense all legal cleanness.
  We apologize for any inconvenience.

• *Corporate elegy:*

C.E.O.:

On behalf of the corporate person
and its subsidiary aisles of flesh,
we travel though antiseptic curtains
today, powered and pancaked, to refresh
our commerce with the dead. We plant a cube
of plastic lilac in the love litter
that the dead make. We sing our lawyers' tune,
a music like money, legal and tender:

"As CEO of self, we always wear
your liability like an orchid
in the foamy meadow of you-know-where."
"As CEO of self, we keep orchards
of freshly laundered factory boys to share.
Just drop by. Our door is always open."

B L A Z O N *(of an undivided sphere)*

scene: they shuttled him beyond—between—the intricate, rented world. And Theas pleads to exhaustion for something to bury: a scarf, a work-glove, a scrap of his overalls. But they will not surrender 'evidence.' So Theas, empty of all but lament:

• *If the self is an articulate knot, then Theas [in sufficiency]:*

I have a kind of self recedes with you.
"Boards-her-in-the-smoke," you call it
with a careful laugh. "Paragon of bruise,"
I say (less with sense than menace).
I have a kind of self exceeds of you,
makes a caesura in the air;
together have a self that eats of you
and leaves the leftovers to share.
Does it dive in a dusk storm? Let it go.
Does it drink wild semaphore all through lunch?
Love, the element where I grow,
is vacancy of you—which space, just touch:
  make me august and still as a frozen lake.
  Make me blithe with you. Make me, still. Please make.

• *If love is a stone anchor (and saying it), then Steelman [in absentia]:*

Please make: spacious and sure, an angle of earth
to compass my bendings, when as I am
I cannot be and wear myself in work
to cease in debt a mouth. To ease, to stand—
and as I am black, unsteady country,
unwork my back to burning and bramble—
and as I am mouth-made-by-voice-to-cease,
make sure and make spacious, earth of angles.
In you is space enough, many in one,
and even your doorstep sings its threshing,
incorporate, barn-built, and plumb,
to make a grammar which maids its singing
  and with small voice makes war on the weather:
  'I am the smoke and the light together.'

S O N G *(seismic butter)*

scene: Theas remains on stage for her signature lament, known to the fans as "Seismic Butter." As the music swells, Theas rises above the stage in a sash of vulcanized rubber. She is coughing up dough. She swings her legs to show her wither-clench and well-laundered apple slices. The crowd pierces the air with their delight.

theas:

tender harness
(if I transcribe

succulent city
the spirit correctly)

he was
god-scent

difficult hour
umbilical bread

chorus:

there was an itch in my forgetting.

the dog bent his ear to it.

he says (all dogs know)

"insoluble technical animal fat."

theas:

he digests
a sliver

a knot
stopped with

root silver
perpetual

from which
length

chorus:

there is a structure of lacking

gone in the teeth

where desire goes

desert of deep influenza

the tender fabric of his stomach
edible mud (or lace thereof)

we know it by its resistance
the portion of thinness which remains.

[While Security gently extracts Theas from the stage, the Chorus joins hands and sings a patriotic song.]

eat like that and you'll get fat
eat like this and you'll be kissed
eat like that and you'll get fat
eat like this and you'll be kissed

[The Chorus repeats this with pride and glee until the coast is clear.]

> *Modern tourists demand to see the highways and streams peopled by shrill, deported women. This is an Arcadian specialty—along with clean hotels and warm, welcoming smiles. However, as evening settles in the private parts of the neighborhood, the police may be asked to clear such women from the places where they loiter. Please remain calm and wait in your rooms. Soon the river will be stiff with juicy shampoo, compliments of the house.*
>
> *—The Management*

ACT FIVE

scene: Foreman's funeral. At intervals during the action—for instance, while the Reverend ascends to the lectern, or as Foreman's Wife (bored or overcome by grief) bends down to fix her nylons and lingers there uncomfortably long, the congregation winding its breath around her—plasticized men, dressed in desert camo, rise from the audience and wander the stage. Their steps are arrested, incomplete. Their uniforms are painted with lime and sand: like a white-washed window they radiate a lymphatic light. They gape at the actors as though trying to speak—but nurses in well-pressed hospital scrubs emerge from the wings of the stage and lead them gently, forcefully, off. The players take no note of these voiceless veterans. The space of the stage should be a point of merger between two entirely distinct realities—one silent, one speaking—co-present in the theater for the space of an act and yet unable to touch each other.

• *Argument:*

"Everything happens as if the poet had wished, in the very act of composition, to demonstrate a fecundity and productive power for which the name of Aphrodite was the wellspring…the maternal and amorous gift of sonorous meat, the diffusion of a fundamental presence through a song of praise."

It does not suffice.

HABEAS CORPUS *(that you might have the body)*

scene: the Chorus gathers before St. Mary of the Lake, the morning of the funeral.

• *The Chorus tests the savors of death:*

Chorus:

Sweet Lizzy Lazarus three days dead,
smokin' a cigar and jumpin' on the bed;
Lizzy on her horse with a hole in her head,
plug it with yr finger or suck out the bread.
Sweet Lazarus, *veni foras*
and show your mega-muscles to the crowd!
Apples to apples, dust to dust:
Lazarus erupts from the golden cloud.
Will you stay, sweet Laz, and wash our cars?
Or take a cookie from the cookie jar?
Adam dared—Adam sat a spell upon the stairs,
and cursed, and cried, "Hey Liz, are you still there?"
"L.'s gone out for cigarettes and coffee!"
"Can't be," says A. "Oh yeah?" says Eve, "It be."

• *notes:*

In this monody, the learned author bewails the death of his friend, once drowned, unfortunately resurrected, and foretells his final assumption when, as he blanches his hoo-ha in the bath, he will be drawn into the heavens, affording us one last look at his ass. We have him—at the zenith of his power, "flames in the forehead of the morning sky"—here in the studio with us; he has asked to address the viewers at home.

[enter Lazarus in sweats and a Bulls jersey, still swaying from last night's libations]: Somewhere something mundane is happening, violently and insistently. (I will not say where.) Somewhere sweet gum paves the antique alleys of your body. Someone there (I will not say who) calls in a dreadful voice: *"Lazare, veni foras* and show your mega-muscles to the crowd. I will tell you a beautiful thing, Lazarus; then I will apologize; then I will tell you a story. Your body is an ellipsis, my body is an ellipsis: melancholy speaks itself."

ESSAY *(on the unmade)*

scene: the Reverend Father; his praise for the dead.

• *"He has risen, just as he said."*

Which grieves, grieves this: habits that ease body
its bodiliness (salt bush and salt blood):
how its accounts are emptied of
the blank senses, gathered to empty.
And pilgrim who sings holy body less
and rents himself, to all the earnest earth,
how opens he, and open learns
borders and blank, the shape of breath.

I mark the edge of him with a blunt pen
so I know else by his not-ness and song.
Was musick'd then, could many song,
this boy whom Circe loved and then—
this wounded shadow which Circe unwove
and weaves in wind. Does it succor? No.

• *"Come and see the place where he lay:"*

Now he is honey in the seams of the rock. Now he rattles like a broken bush. The space where he was ripeness and bird shivers and starts away. He resolves to water even as he rises from it. He unlocks even as he offers himself to be bound. So we say with one voice, which populates our several throats:

the granite is
differenced

only by heat
from the river

that wears it away
it is sown

a natural body
it is raised

PETITION *(for all things, a living music)*

scene: the congregation joins its many voices to a single space: to police. to presence. to lift the bruise from its shackle in the blood.

•

Is lifted in thought—is furnished in it:
is border-barked and presence bound. (Then what?)
It must wear out—must cleanly house and limb
its aging in things—which will its will unknot:
though I feel its envy rub, garlic tough,
accident named, "Song and Stuff." (And then what?)
It must wear out—must seek an end to love:
is tissue-barked and lifted into thought.
Long is riverhead—makes a morning rut.
Do not ask what good it does: it knows how
to go on—makes an end of love. (Then what?)
Then lift the coal, o man of unclean mouth
and write—write his name where the rail rubbed
  it out. Perishing road and opened ground,
  he is lifted in voice. Then make a mournful sound.

• *"And they came and held him by the feet:"*

That he rejoices chiefly in music, we know by oak and asp. That he rejoices in beaten matter, we know by the music it makes in the grass. Still his sorrow will not soften. Still we taste the bitter mortar in the heart of things. Therefore we say, with a single voice: the spirit that is / does not build up / nature around us / but puts it forth / through us / artery / a curtain / a turn in winter / as the life of trees / puts forth new branches / and leaves / through the pores of the old:

But it differs
from the flesh

in one important
respect:

it is a fixed point
whereby

we may measure
our departure.

INVOCATION *(to the waters)*

scene: the Reverend Father addresses the crew of mourners.

• *orison*

Reverend: From which the mud-sick mother, desolate
   and quick, rises to tend her things:
   rough eglantine, tattered cowslip,
pitcher of bees, to which she swerves and sinks.
   And once she was shatter and thrum,
a cold voice, unweaving. And once she lent
   her tattered edge to salve the drum:
still the skin sinks and longing has its length.

When river-drunk, belly-burst—when tooth gouged
   her frigid hand and harrowed book—
when swerved in tempest turn—she finger-plowed
   her furrow to ask where it took
its lapse, its whetstone ash, the liquid edge
from which she rose—still, it passes knowledge.

• *notes:*

There is an obstruction here,
some excess of phlegm.

POST SCRIPT *(with news of the author's miraculous rebirth)*

scene: exeunt omnes, piously. The stage returns, slowly, to its original bareness: populated now by the angel of luxurious cardboard and his dog. Who ordered these stand-up comedians? Who supplied them with a cheese tray and drink tickets? Every angel is boring. In the distance, I see a figure of celestial singleness come to purge our English stage.

• *From the laureate hearse, dressed in the blank part of the text, and sweating profusely, Toby or not Toby (and thinking makes him so):*

Toby:

When to an elsewhere alcove of honey,
I summon up dark Easter of things past,
from its refuge in tense and avid grass—
deep and exact, an imperial jelly—
then I open to chemical weather,
the fresh elision native to the place;
then I house polluted geese in my face.
I'm wearing their water now. And a sweater.

All spring, time touching himself. Carnally.
He, like, likes sex, but loves the law.
He is thought on wings of grease and rubs it raw.
He is debt sap, and knows it. Partially.
"Gosh I am the hot liquor of things past!"
he says and drinks the thing he is. And lacks.

• *He marches through the crowd, with candy for the critics, kisses for the kids. All together, they sing:*

Despite the endfulness / of life / there remains / a reservoir of creature / uncertain fence / heavy with speech / and unspoiled / by sex / its scent in all cities / its home in none / the clay ridge / [of a tiled roof] / where language / is the hows of being / insufficient / even to a headache / and comprised of /

scented bladder / and stony passage / suffused in brand: / blind the guide / who delights in law / until the act / becomes / bearable / and from his wound / insatiable design / a blossom in the spleen /

the same principle / is at work / in the groin / of several mountains / in such a way / that / we ask after / its pungent absence / for the pleasure / of the patients: / the [more]… the [more]… / which gives itself / to be said /

SONG *(a ruined must)*

scene: up jumps the Poet and shakes the sleep from his flush and fragrant bodice. Today the earth is new made! The evening's storm of violence has left sewers in the mud—soft-mealed, liquid mud—which he travels, sucking up the sugar. His sense is drenched. All day, tender as boiled beef, he and his Verb laugh and sing and bruise their poor, perishable I. Living check to check in filthy rented rooms, this I is a confection of liquid knots, soft, articulate with the law. When, at last, the time is ripe and gourmandized, the I looses its long lament against the Poet:

•

I: consider
the bone
as pure
mechanism
silica disk
and rotary
brush

where cold
makes
the tongue
a frame
against
black sewing

gathered
in the teeth

is the name
of want
an idiom
of is and isn't

is sought
only a ribbon
of sex
the fact
of which
is almost
music

isn't is
an accusation
against
migratory cough
tender industrial
fabric
milky industrial
sex

[exit Poet and Verb, pursued by insatiable I.]

DELETED SCENES (a satyr play)

scene: Oedipus and the Sphinx lounging in the ballroom of an unfinished hotel, where several major corporations are negotiating: to make him tender, small and distant—a family man. As it is, the corporate person is turned on by this moist, ungoverned spectacle. It demands to shed its lingerie. Unclothed, it is more sublime than nation itself. "Let's make a plague there!" say the corporations and point at Oedipus. "Not to be," says Oedipus (after some work with his analyst), "That would do me good." Then Oedipus wagers a winik.

•

"just a-
round the corner is another corner!"
(Bernstein)

• *Argument:*

Stern is the meat that eats, stern the jail from which the soul bursts in funeral clothes, stern the warden's dogs that drag it back. Aristotle, always the voyeur, hangs above the earth from a luxurious noose and smirks. Tell me, Aristotle, what the backbone of empire backs. And Aristotle says: "One wishes to be consummated by nation. Wrapped in the used bandages of nation, one blisters and sings excitedly in the coffee shop. Because one has been to college. Because one's father raised fighting cocks. (Cocks fight and this is called narrative). Over carcasses of industrial chicken, the nation picks its dialects with an enormous thighbone and laughs and calls you a Jew. You will learn that the nation is fluent in nothing but narrative—though it denies it fluently, persistently, at every cocktail party to anyone who will listen."

SEX SCENE *(theory of tragedy)*

scene: Theas and Foreman seal the deal.

• *If I am that name:*

Chorus: Under her antibiotic umbrella:
a silky sheet of televised snow.
Where she goes, ecstasy and distemper:
she's sick with knowing, not the thing she knows.
Theas: Behind the armor of deodorant,
I am abscess and respite, swerved:
the living joy that gives its government
to pleasure and its toxins to the nerve.
Pregnant with its lapse, I exact
the chewy marble buried in his eye;
I ask the spitting image—leg askance,
leaking muteness, for all the boys to ride—
to lift the past from the chemical thatch
of her underpants.
Foreman: Can I quote you on that?

• *Applause and laughter. Theas lifts her dress and lies face down on the bed. Fade to black. After a long, liquid pause, enter Oedipus and the Sphinx, thus overgrown, thus richly mulched:*

O: I want a verse that hurts the thing it says. In an infectious and unwholesome country, I sing *love is good enough for what it does* and check my makeup in a pocket mirror. I want a verse that shows its sex, delicate as a pair of loafers, to the mirror. I want a verse that makes a moist wound environment and plumps itself with sheets of fun and flirty teeth. I want a verse that eats a bonny bed pan, full of foam. O mournful rivers of hamburger meat, I want a verse that bathes its acne in vivid soda. I want a verse that weighs its heinie with apple pie and climbs into bed. I want a verse that brews its cancered fruit in the dead ground and rises through the living room to get a shot of water. Today the lawn is arrayed in rough hexameters to tempt the mower. I want a verse that comes to the mowing like a virgin touched for the very first time: pure bliss, no errata, unlimited text and data.

S: I want doesn't get.

LIVE INTIMATE NOSTALGIA *(theory of tragedy)*

scene: Steelman—in a frenzy of knowing—asks his Daddy for advice.

• *"If I've killed one man, I've killed two"*

Steelman:

If my money is a loaf of cancer,
which walks through flesh and butters what it likes,
if it radiates plastic from its bladder,
the brick and mortgaged idiom of rights;
if time is ruined meat: the panting bowel
implicit with oil—the dark continents
of grief—policed by the ecstatic muscle,
which bind its substance to a liquid fence—

Daddy:

then I went out to the pasture to say
the unbearable weight of things on thought.
These days devour memory. They break
the delicate envelope of things. They cost
  a pocket full of proses. Ashes, ashes:
  O rapt pasture, show me where the cash is.

• *Enter Oedipus and the Sphinx, tenderly clothed in genre:*

O: I went out in the raw season to pay back taxes to the pasture. Here [*points at his bosom*] the dead are leached of their longing by sweet industrial laundries. Here the dead rise up and press themselves into the groin of genre: humming and spent, wet with division. You are their mascot for the two hours traffic of our stage.

S: Wrong-o, Keebler.

O: All the plow-month, I spoke words chosen in desire: shaved and incontinent, language under a cloud of language. In the myth, there are many kinds of sensuous fake meat on which the dead feast: Sahara meat lovers combination for two; anchovy salad with hot chunks of the nude. In the myth, the brows and breasts of the dead are painted with ash, to mark them as the viral atom of wanting: the crisp nothing it gathers as.

S: I'm afraid I'll be of no more help to you goodbye.

THEORY OF TRAGEDY *(crossroads of america)*

• *scene: Foreman pawns his pureloined tissues.*

Foreman:

Dressed in Daddy's optic white and cargoed
with forgotful light, I rise, exhausted,
from this star-spangled nest, this sorrowed
hill of flesh, which was my native office.
Now the emptiness set in and it always do.
O HELL IS TIME it says and sticks its time
in my temporal crevice. It gives the brute
pastoral power at work inside these lines.

All our delighted spirits are dripping fat
and I count myself a delighted one:
unleased and sugar-free, wet and well-hung.
And yet death missed its exit. So I sat
in Indiana, with ankle unstrung,
waiting for its edible silence to come.

• *As though summoned by the word "Indiana," the Sphinx pours onto the stage, perfumed and posed. She composes her face as she takes off her clothes. "Don't you want to see my special underwear?" she asks. We want to see her special underwear. "Don't you want to touch me where I am undivided water?" We want to touch her where she is undivided. We want to taste the gooey excrement of time. We want to wipe the mud and musk from her bones. To market her meat space as chemical bread. What we want, she butchers and serves with soda and chicken salad, fresh from the fridge in her leasing office. Genital chaos is come again—this time at bargain basement prices! She winks at us and brings Foreman a dish of her freshest stuff. While he lounges in the showroom, drenched in factory scent, she folds his golden melancholy laundry and puts it away for good. All the while, he soliloquizes to the Romans and shows off his scars:*

Even in death I live a very rich life I'm fit and tan here I am barfing in a hotel the color of dank and woeful prairie. Even in death, I make sweet lunch to the dizzy air—o lush lewd air that spreads like a Ziploc bag for every prying hand! O that our too too salad flesh would melt and resolve itself to a matching bra and pantie set! "What is man?" I asked the angel, and the angel said, "Debt." "See to your rents, boy," he said. He showed his liquid organs, his shawl of wind, his commodious thing. Fainting, I follow where he goes: dark suburban streets, undiscovered countries, where the deer and the buffalo roam.

Even in death, his ass sweats secretly in summer. Even in death, he laughs and says "HYR PWR LOLLLLL." "Boy I am hungry for sorrow," he says. He calls to his bros where they crouch in the audience waiting to back him up. They have smeared their private parts in polluted mud. They wear a canopy of fat, nuclear roses in their hair. They enter erect and newly baroque, singing their national anthem. Thank God this kind of poem harms no one! Thank God their livers and brains are perfectly preserved by air conditioning and tanning salts for the anatomy class!

all, singing:	Fat fish are happy fish
	Skinny fish are sad!
	Fat fish are happy fish
	Skinny fish are sad!
1st Arcadian:	**im a happy fish**
all:	MOLOCH IS IN ME
2nd Arcadian:	**im a sad fish**
all:	MOLOCH IS IN ME
3rd Arcadian:	**hes eating my lungs out**
all:	HE CAN PUT ANYTHING IN HIS MOUTH
4th Arcadian:	**hes a government man now**
all:	HE CAN PUT EVERYTHING IN HIS MOUTH
	Fat fish are happy fish
	Skinny fish are sad!
	Fat fish are happy fish
	Skinny fish are sad!
Sphinx:	That's what she said.

• We find ourselves, briefly, in an abstract space: the tiled womb of a Burger King; the pleasant pastures of Arcadia; a talk show which entertains the dead while they crouch in their dirty offices snared in paperwork. Foreman is led on stage, his edible stuff a gathering was. And the host, robed in denim shorts and aviator shades (better to show his delicious musculature—though his substance itself is an illusion produced by certain proprietary vapors), asks: "Now that you've vaulted past it, what was your meat and muscle?" And Foreman answers:

A glass of milk without the milk—
an engine of absence, and/or
difficult oil; a solemn door
which fills with tissue and builds
a narrow curtain in the breath—
what Kant calls erkenntnis: cleaning
of the graves, a cavernous eating,
O and I; I and O—what else:
it clings to its portion of thinness,
man-sized; a rank and crusted house;
it gives its fragrance to the couch
and takes its depth from rigid inches;
  two birds, one stone: something endowed
  with want alone: something withstood.

BEST PRACTICES *(theory of tragedy)*

scene: the Chorus and C.E.O. of Arcadia Steel discuss their public relations strategy.

•

Chorus: Where we go a-gargling sweet and spermy
data—a bulb of cameras overhead
and plastic in the water—we said
with corporate pleasure, lovely, dark, and deep:
"Ummmmm no comment. God will supply the want
(though in a pinch, of course, our brand will do).
He moves on the face of our revenue:
the glad contract that makes our money meant."

C.E.O.: Our brand is a frail and fatty vessel:
a varicose sack of departed acts
or whatever. Go to the dead and ask
for quality time and a bowl of pretzels.

Chorus: We did. But they were out to lunch. Alone.
And Time said, with feeling, "Throw me a bone."

• *Oedipus and the Sphinx, prolific as pornography:*

O: Tragedy is a desiccated animal
Tragedy is a conduit for capital
Tragedy is a rope of liquid soap
Tragedy is a thrust of stone through stone
Tragedy is field noise and work against the spine
Tragedy is the style of desire particular to time
Tragedy is the unplowed fingers of the dead
which linger in the thing you said
Tragedy is language and the weather
rubbing their lard together
Tragedy is the surplus of sleep aid
which lingers under our author's blouse
Tragedy is the soft weather of summer, an arcade
which makes its country in the mouth
Tragedy is the compact and gerrymandered essence
which gives the self and its lesions
The grass is grieving and the waters doubled
Tragedy in its greasy limousine grins and rides the bubble

S: Close. But no cigar.

ARCADIAN MUSCLE *(theory of tragedy)*

scene: the Abominations gather at the bar to hymn their fallen bro.

• *On a buoyant pillow of oohs and aahs, their bushel of voice rises and sinks:*

Abominations:

When all his fragrance unfolds on the bed
and the wet cement in his undershirt
gives contractual abundance to the lead-
lined casket that we framed to house his hurt,
when the poet's eye is a choral eye
and breeds a basket of fresh, toxic bread
for his language to lunch, and when he lies
undressed by all the eating hours, fled
from himself with a shudder in the loins,
then—too late—he sets himself aside.
You set yourself aside. You lay a coin
upon your lips to pay the ghostly ride.
You light the bright, moral bulbs where you flee.
The poem harvests your transparency.

• *Enter Oedipus. He carries the Sphinx, like a mattress, strapped to his back. She is perjured and vacuumed, black blood threaded through her face and eyes. This quintessence of debt, this slim-fast youth with all her juice pressed to an elegant perfume! Her contract is up. Where she is not tied down, she erupts like a drunken cop toward the tax havens in the poem. Oedipus, made light by love, sings to her in his surgical way.*

O: The dead do not eat the grave. They are out gathering orchids in far fields of Thessaly. They are eating combo meals in the basement of the Pentagon McDonald's. Today, I say—they have flowered! The hole in the heart of the geranium bed, which even yesterday I massaged with bleach and tanning oil, is liquid with feeling: desolate fences and frostbitten apples which erupt through the navel, singing, "Your body is a wonderland." O, I have taken too little care of this! I scare myself with my own dessert places. Am I not viscous and abundant, an ambulatory sludge? Don't I sing in the marsh weeds on behalf of eternal love? Indeed, every fishmonger suffers thus. Every housewife keeps rigid potato salad against the day when, on a violent surfboard, someone silent comes to rinse the meat out of her meaning, first with his pearly taser and later with his gun—

S: Bummer.

SONG *(post-mortem: a televised spectacular)*

scene: a tv studio in the bowels of Arcadia. Enter Theas, guarded by generic male voices. She waves and smiles and flees to the couch where her dead wait, anxious to be rinsed in spaceless chemicals. (Such rinsing never ceases.) It is the hour when the Chorus engages in ravenous smooching. Coiffed in spirit and digesting its storm, enter the anchor, chanting the theme song of his show: "It's time to convert all your fear and joy / into surplus value, an IPO." He is the beloved and bad business boy. He honors the invisible hands that paint the body blank. "Now Theas," he says in a voice glad and lack, "Let's talk about you. Is it sensuous concrete or the draining of?" He laughs and pats her hand.

theas: the revenant / mare / the surge of / sex / specific to the ox. / this is what thinking does: / it stretches / its secret law / to the field / like a lover, it is a savage grammar / like a lover it leaves / dark favors in the bed / a scarf / a ball of wire / a secret bruise / beneath the skirt

anchor: think of us as becoming, not being. you see, for instance, the soft steam of sorrow which melts out of our ears: evergreen and azalea, co-present in the word. each night we renovate the toothsome caverns. from the lime of the earth, where the apple was, translated to ruin:

chorus: love is easier than you think
its savage eating its savage eating

Ezekiel saw / his eye / against the Is. / (sharp sage rough / tinder) / it gave / astonished / to be // burnt // it names its difficult species / of desire / spring cancer / (name of names) / we know it by its resistance / the history of which / is like a long caress /

we who pressure to know unclothed and sublime fortification. we who were intimate as the landscape to his folding and unfolding: we delight in all forms of wounding. (in such synthesis the labor ends.)

chorus:

love is easier than you think
its savage eating its savage eating

has the world so slept / fixed stem / within the ear / infected with / supposedly / or / deprived / of buoyancy / young time / called shepherd's needle? /

all together, singing:

O Zeus alone awake , making plums
had this way of evening his damaged
hand his bare device in lucid music
lawful as eating lawful as eating
lawful as eating lawful as eating
lawful as eating lawful as eating
lawful as eating lawful as eating
lawful as eating lawful as eating
lawful as eating lawful as eating
lawful as eating lawful as eating
lawful as eating lawful as eating
lawful as eating lawful as eating
lawful as eating lawful as eating
lawful as eating lawful as eating

note how a play always ends with an exit. the genre demands a loss of presence. therefore, a portion of their thinness remains on stage chanting indefinitely.

Note on Performance:

The text of this play is unfinished, even empty. It demands actors, landscapes, readers who intervene, I hope, violently. True, the play provides some instructions for how you might do that. I would like you to think of those instructions as punishments or impositions. I want to encourage you to ignore me, to drown my book. For instance, you might:

1) Feed this book through a paper shredder with your tax returns and receipts. Burn the shreds and scatter the ashes at your local superfund site. Invite your friends to a picnic on a landfall. Perform the play there from memory until your memory or your body is exhausted.

2) Repeat each line between seventeen and three hundred times.

3) Erase the word *body* wherever it appears in the play. Perform the play otherwise as written but obscure the actors behind a semi-translucent screen, so that their bodies are only intermittently visible.

4) Perform the play in total silence.

5) Give up around act three and go out for a drink.

6) Perform the play alone, in the solitude of a closed room. It's a summer day and the air conditioning's off. Your face is a field of sweat. You produce a strange, strangled sound, "the spontaneous overflow of powerful feeling." Now how did all that money get in your mouth?

Acknowledgments:

Poems from this manuscript have previously appeared in the following journals and anthologies: *Best American Experimental Writing 2014*, *Black Warrior Review*, *Crazyhorse*, *Cream City Review*, *Diagram*, *Fact-Simile*, *Gigantic Sequins*, *Industrial Lunch*, *The Laurel Review*, *Liens*, *The Offending Adam*, *Parallax*, *Phantom Limb*, *Sporklet*, *Tammy*, *Tinge*, and *Whiskey Island*.

Greying Ghost Press published a selection from this book, *Tender Industrial Fabric*, in 2015. I was able to finish and polish the manuscript thanks to residencies from the Vermont Studio Center and the Millay Colony for the Arts.

This book was composed through extravagant acts of plagiarism and theft. I stole anything that wasn't bolted to the ground. To those who love privacy, subjectivity, and property, I apologize sincerely. My thoughts and prayers are with you and your loved ones. I have long since forgotten most of the sites and sources that I stole from, so in lieu of an exhaustive bibliography, I will just mention the titles that come to mind: Shakespeare's *Sonnets*, Milton's *Paradise Lost*, *Firefly*, Taylor Swift, "Back to December," Kyd, *The Spanish Tragedy*, "Lycidas," Frank Kermode's intro to *The Selected Poems of Andrew Marvell*, Toni Morrison, *Sula*, Plath, "Daddy," John Berryman, *Sonnets to Chris*, Brecht, "The Swamp," Virginia Woolf, *Mrs. Dalloway*, John Mayer, "Your Body is a Wonderland," Sina Queryas, *MxT*, Margaret Fuller, Emerson, Jon Woodward's *Uncanny Valley*, some parts of *The Bible*...

My enduring gratitude to all of the actors, directors, and curators who helped me stage parts of this play over the years: Nathan Hoks, Emily Barton Altman, Denise Dooley, Adrienne Dodt, Mel Bentley, Kimberley Ann Southwick, Liana Katz, Paul Siegell, Jacob Bennett, Jen Brown, Mike Lala, Allyson Paty, Sophie Herron, Hannah Aizenman, Ira Murfin, Kate Morris, Hannah Keene, Udita Upadhyay, Casey Caldwell, Eleanor Russell, Will Pierce, Lee Benjamin Huttner, Laura Goldstein, Catherine Theis, Tyler Crumrine, Magus Magnus, Cean Gamalinda, Jennifer Karmin, Gwyneth Anderson, Nathaniel Lee Jones, David Pritchard, Christopher Schaeffer, Andy Robinson, Jack Kovacs, Nik De Dominic, and Christine Larusso. I know I've forgotten some of you and I'm sorry.

This play was a collaborative endeavor from the start, drawing on the conversation, counsel, and energy of people who I love and admire. I remain grateful to you for your work and your friendship. Thank you: Emily Barton Altman, Mel Bentley, Jay Besemer, Tyler Crumrine, Alexander Dickow, Nick Demske, Adrienne Dodt, Johannes Göransson, Reginald Gibbons, Laura Goldstein, Jennifer Karmin, Mary Kinzie, Sophie Klahr, Mike Lala, Jess Lee, Allyson Paty, David Pritchard, Prageeta Sharma, Kimberley Ann Southwick, Alix Anne Shaw, Gene Tanta, and Andrew Wessels.

I started writing this play alongside Emily Barton Altman—some of the earliest pieces of it come from a collaborative sonnet sequence we worked on for a while called, aptly enough, "Sonnets to Orifice." This play emerges from a deep intermingling of our creative energies, our language, our capacities for grief and love. It is dedicated to her. As Denise Levertov writes, "It is you who make / a world to speak of."

TOBY ALTMAN is the author of *Arcadia, Indiana* (Plays Inverse, 2017) as well as five chapbooks, including recently *Security Theater* (Present Tense Pamphlets, 2016). His poems can be found in *Crazyhorse*, *Jubilat*, *Lana Turner*, and other journals and anthologies. He is currently completing a PhD in English at Northwestern University. In the Fall of 2017, he will begin an MFA in poetry at the Iowa Writers Workshop.